ISBN-13:978-1539178163

ISBN-10:1539178161

THE ABC's COLORING BOOK WITH ANIMALS AND PROFESSOR HOGAN.

Hi Kids! I'm Professor Hogan.
The Most Intelligent Dog In the World!

Let's learn the ABC's and Color the Animals.

A a

A is for Antelope.

Antelope

B b

B is for Bear.

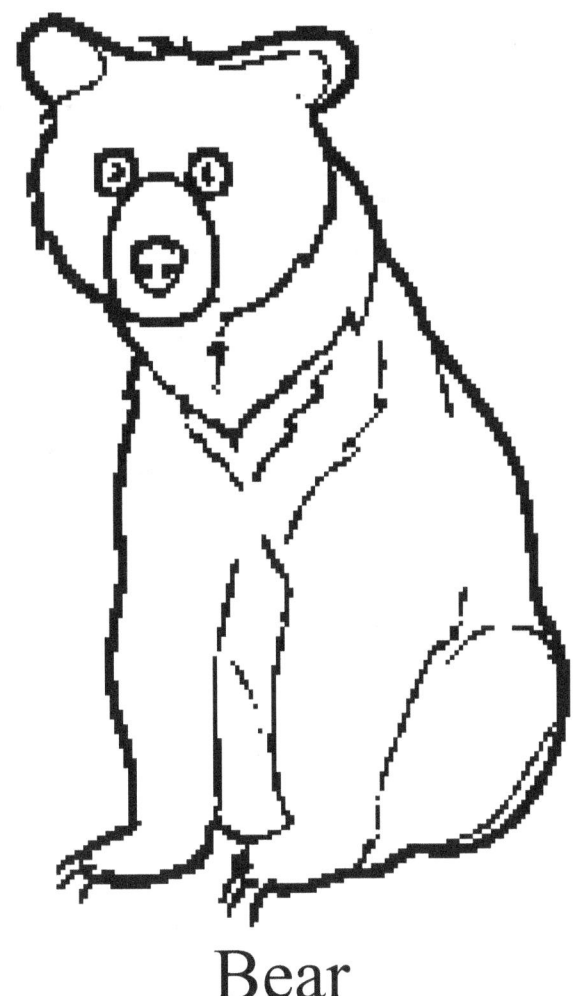

Bear

C c

C is for Cat.

Cat

D d

D is for Dog.

Dog

E e

E is for Elephant.

Elephant

F f

F is for Fox.

Fox

G g

G is for Gorilla.

Gorilla

H h

H is for Hawk.

Hawk

I i

I is for Impala.

Impala

J j

J is for Jackal.

Jackal

K k

K is for Kangaroo.

Kangaroo

L l

L is for Lion.

Lion

M m

M is for Moose.

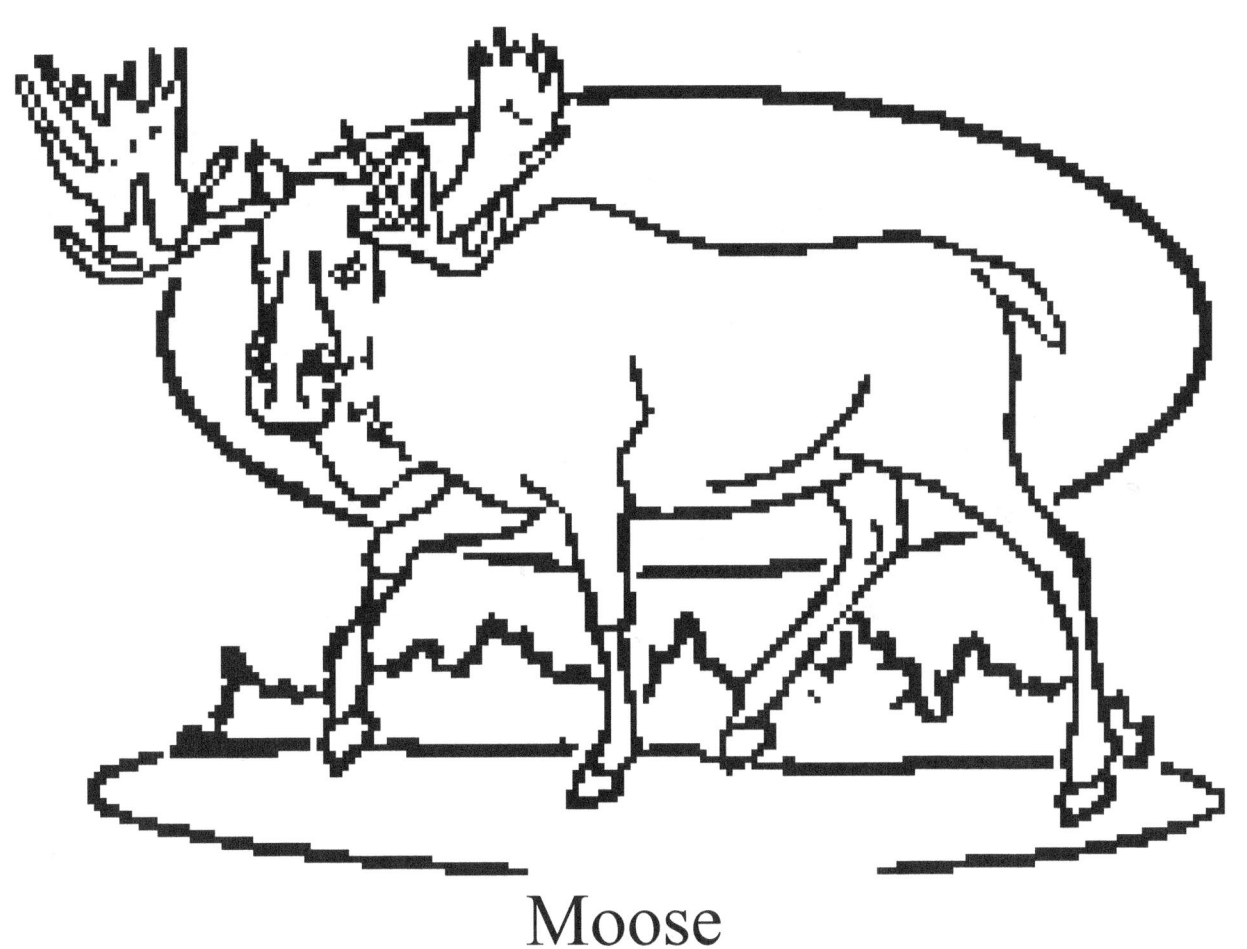

Moose

N n

N is for Newt

Newt

O o

O is for Owl.

Owl

P p

P is for Porcupine.

Porcupine

Q q

Q is for Quail.

Quail

R r

R is for Raccoon.

Raccoon

S s

S is for Stork.

Stork

T t

T is for Tiger.

Tiger

U u

U is for Uakari.

Uakari

V v

V is for Vulture.

Vulture

W w

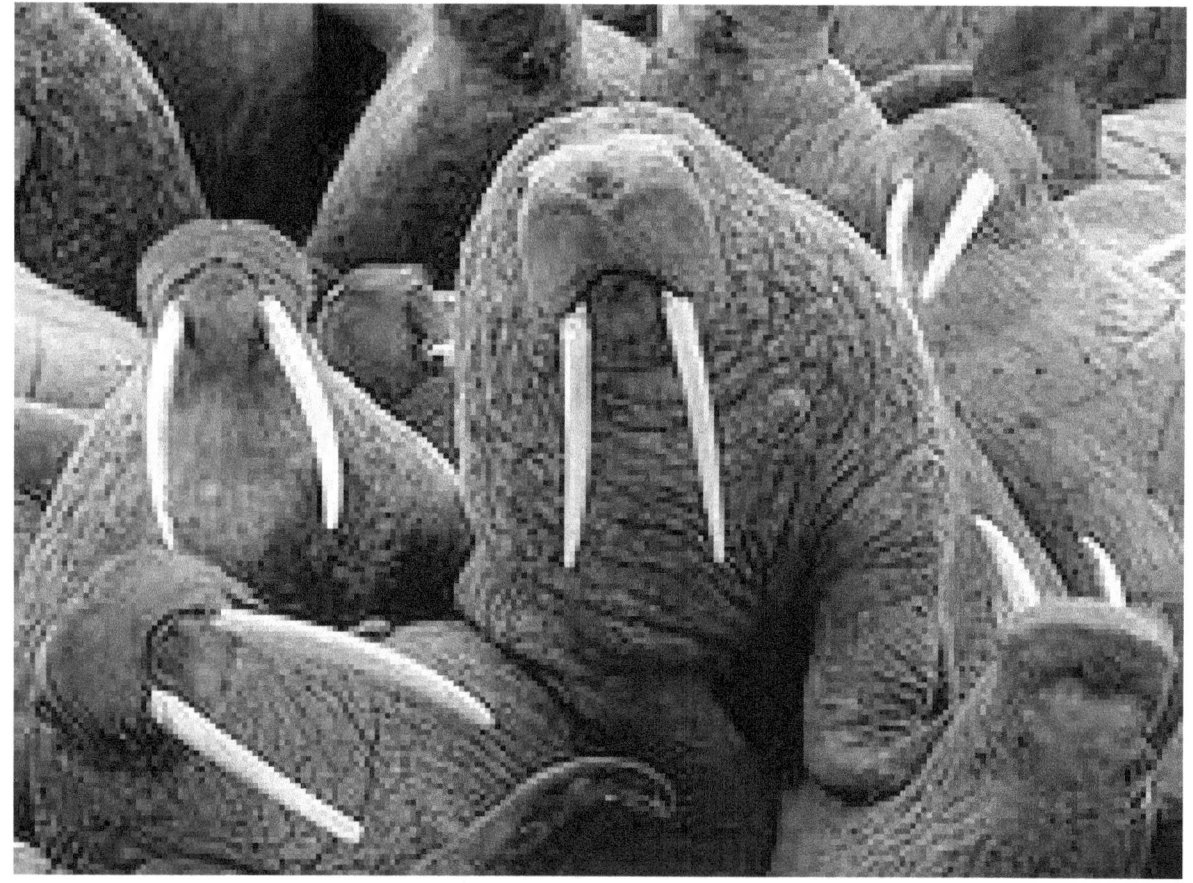

W is for Walrus.

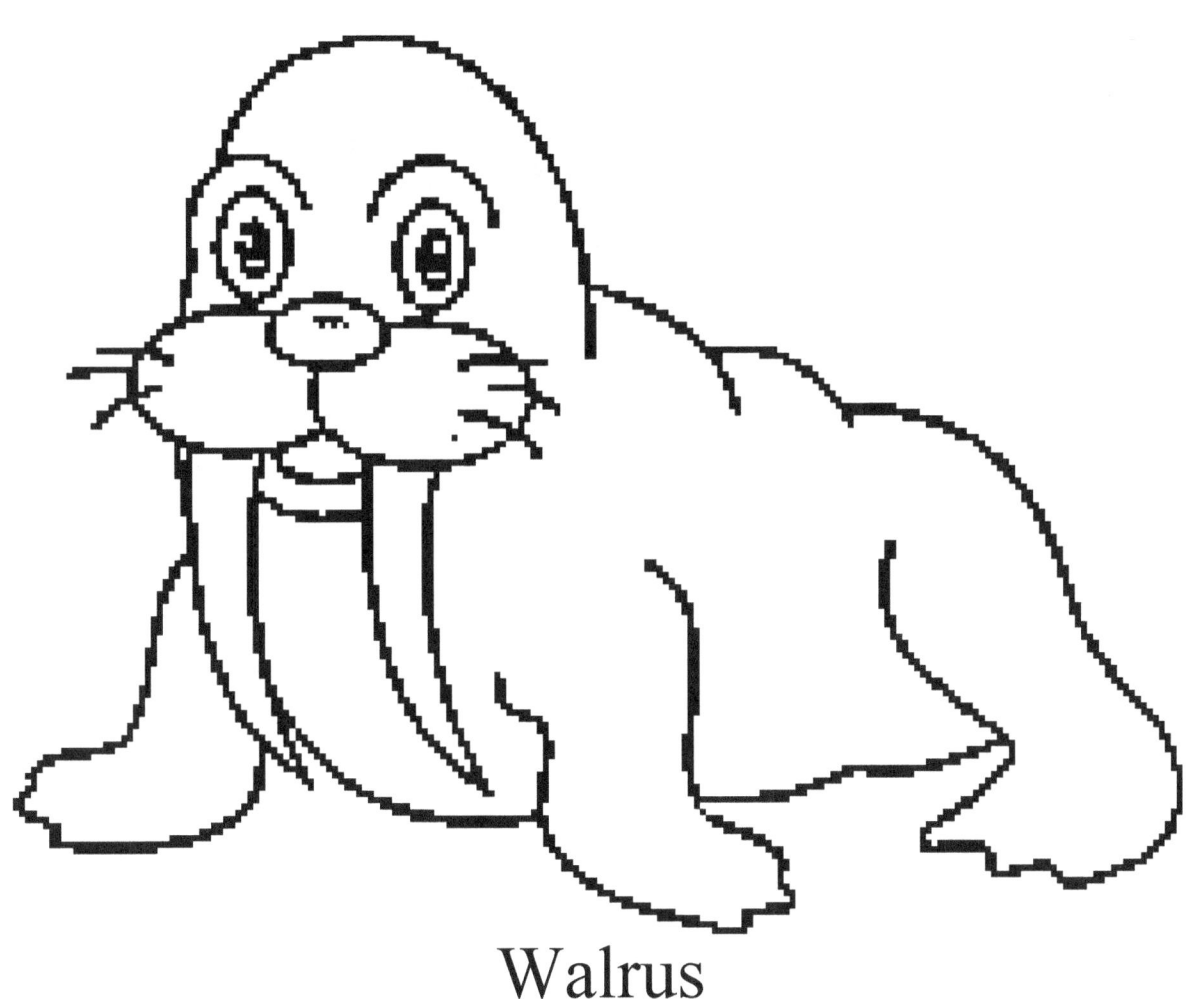

Walrus

X x

X is for Xantus Hummingbird.

Xantus Hummingbird

Y y

Y is for Yak.

Yak

Z z

Z is for Zebra.

Zebra

Very Good!

Now Let's Repeat the ABC's.

ABCDEFGH
IJKLMN
OPQRSTUV
WXYZ

THAT WAS FUN!
SEE YOU SOON.
YOUR FRIEND, PROFESSOR
HOGAN.

GOODBYE

www.ingramcontent.com/pod-product-compliance
Lightning Source LLC
Chambersburg PA
CBHW081748280526

45789CB00008B/2777